a language only the earth remembers.

kat.

isbn 979-8-9939728-0-0

dedication.

to ancestors and the moon,
to the girl i was, and the woman i'm becoming.

to the pine trees and the planets,
and the rock that lies below them.

ineffable.

oh you rebel child,
you make poets rage at their paper and pens,
for ornate words cannot begin to describe
how the universe conspired to dream you into being.

awaken.

2

a burden of consciousness,
a gift or a curse.

can you still be awake
and remain human?

silence.

i open my mouth to speak,
yet only silence escapes my lips.
panic begins to settle in my throat,
heart flutters like a caged bird in my chest.
stomach swirling, ritual in motion.

ground, ground, sit in the silence.

what i was not prepared for
was being comfortable in stillness.

time.

fragments of memory flash before stars,
beyond space, slipping lucidly
through my fingers,
falling softly like rain.

where rain lands, flowers bloom.
moved by a gentle, passing breeze,
caressing each petal as if they were known to them,
whispering reminders that this is temporary, subtle.
but even time is not moved by it.

not moved by our shadowed footsteps,
brief, gentle, voices faint,
echoes within the wind,
carrying divine breath on fingertips.
moving without care, worry, rearranging the ground
beneath us
until, we too, are swept away.

i look up to the moon,
wondering if it recognizes my ancestors in my face.
soft light, faint, constant,
warm on my skin.
slips away like it never truly belonged to me.

the petals recognize its embrace
and bloom anyway.

time embraced gently within my hands,
delicate, slipping between breaths,
carried away in the wind.
i release a sigh of surrender
as rivers carve their own paths
through walls of rock and stone.
even they know the futility of stillness.

moon.

it's been a while since i've seen you,

        i know, she responds, *and it's not the clouds*
                        that hid me away.

she bows down low to meet my gaze,
waxing crescent, sentient being,
she sees my tired eyes and sighs,

                        why are you trying so hard?

i gaze hazily back, expressionless,
she knows me too well,
of all the evenings i've looked up at her,
a child once dreaming of flying,
the adult dazing in silent nights,
to her, my thoughts are a canvas of colors,
abstract and yet knowing,
full abundance.

her ethereal light wraps around me,
quiet, tender,
not lost, just still,
a shawl woven of shadow and silver,
each thread a memory i once tried to forget,

but she holds them like heirlooms,
softly, so they don't shatter.
waning mother, old friend.

breathe, and just be,

she hums in the stillness,
like a hymn without sound,
and i remember i am still holy,
even when i feel hollow.

i am tired, i reply, but she knows.
there are feelings i haven't spoken out loud in years,
and i realize it's not just her i miss,
but the ones who used to call me by my name.
i want to talk to angels and ancestors,
god and the moon

eclipse.

keep my face hidden
from wandering eyes,
for if beauty is the underling of one's desire,
stoked beneath the magma of passion,

how cursed must one be
to be as prepossessing as the sun,

and yet
so misunderstood?

war.

long before the earth split with division,
beneath the sound and weight of marching feet,
there was silence.
earth tender with life, trees of old,
bent gently, not with sorrow, but with life,
watching children play under their branches,
starry-eyed, limitless dreamers.
the trees gifted them leaves upon their hair,
and dewed grass upon their mother's feet.
a time when rivers remembered only songs,
and not blood.

divided men, holding banners stitched from pride,
mouths full of promise, eyes empty of love,
force-fed beliefs, stomachs aching for a filling
that will never come.
a tyrant beckons the call, fat on his throne,
spitting false glory as if it were rain,
and we were dehydrated, thirsty.
yet they did not notice the rot that grew underneath.

the trees trembled first, not from the wind,
but from assembled machines that do not weep.
golden grain devoured with flame, death,
the sky split open, aching, heavy with fire,

the moon watching helplessly as her daughters cry.
she calls out to the children, *run, run, run.*
the child whispering playfully to the wind,
not knowing it could carry smoke instead of song.

marching feet, burning towers, the jester laughs,
dancing on the soot of broken dreams.
mothers turn to stone, fathers to ash,
children learning the sound of silence,
all for the glory of who is right.
but who are we to say what is?
the king sits on his throne, wine and caviar,
while the children choke on ashes of their loved ones.

empty forests, soleless feet, hopeless,
trembling with fear and devastation.
it was god's plan, the king muses,
his court agrees, the jester dances on.
yet somewhere beyond space and time,
beyond the cries of the wind, bite of the sun, tears of the
rain,
god weeps.

iridescent.

white feathered moth,
iridescent, descending
through heavy wind, she flies,
not caring where the breeze takes her.
no worry of the harsh sun on her back,
only the gentle push of her wings,
the sweet sound of freedom,
riding through the chaos,
with no worry where she's going,
only where she is.

projection.

night lift me higher into the velvet sky,
may my feet no longer touch the earth,
toes gracing the ecstasy of the universe.
take me back to this astral field,
where i was consumed in light years of stars,
a galaxy that could barely fill
the hunger within my tired soul.

take my body back to the dirt i was created from.
use me as a vessel, cradled within the aura
of the blood moon,
fingers caressing the rings of saturn.
i chase the creation of you through constellations,
yet i feel your soul touch mine.
infectious infection, divine intoxication,
the taste of you lingering on my lips,
along with all the words i've wanted to say,
and didn't.

balancing delicately on four limbs,
razor blade ecstasy lacing my tongue
in a language only the stars remember.
no longer on the ground, i project
higher than my higher self,

complacent within the silent heavens.
do i dare wake up?

13

fourteen.

there you are, all but fourteen,
petals barely bloomed along your face,
and yet they already tried to burn you.
the war on the outside is no place for a child,
yet you wear the scars so well
for someone so gentle.

it is so like you
to gather the broken pieces with your light
and shine in the darkest of places,
to radiate love, in trust, and in kindness,
and they noticed. they always do.
they noticed your starlit eyes,
and thought to take them from you,
as if the fire they stole from you,
could warm the coldness that plagues them.

little fawn, I know you cry when you're alone.
I know you think your kindness a weakness
and wish the anger to swallow you whole,
to become the monster they tried to make you.
but, darling, your gentleness is rebellion,
your softness a weapon
sharpened in the dark.

half gods require milk and honey,
real gods require blood.

let your sorrow teach you song,
let your words become poetry,
bleeding from your lips on paper.
you dream of being something colder,
something that doesn't bleed when touched.
you think your kindness is weakness,
what will one day undo you,
but my dear, achilles was like the sun
you were always the moon

genesis.

16

my sisters grow wary
of an ominous creature
with two arms and two legs.
a creature to whom we were taught
that we were born from its rib.

creation.

what am i, god,
if not to be unnamed?
a descendant carried within
your own creation,
a child with doe-like eyes
and an innocent smile,
trying to discern the meaning
behind the direction of the wind,
behind every feather from a dove's wing,
the number of crows in the field.

what divine purpose is that of
the maiden, the priestess,
but to look for you in the starlit sky,
and surrenders willfully to its beauty?
do you not see the longing in her eyes
and think how beautiful it is
to create something so delicate,
so passionate in seeking divine truth,
so loving, that every monster and angel
falls in love at first sight?

where am i, god of the angel armies,
if not in the arms of the earth mother,
goddess of soft pines and maples,

finding refuge within the wildflowers?
no one kingdom apart from another,
one whole place you call heaven.
altair, flying eagle,
carry this ache of mine across the sky.
i quietly pray for the solace to find me,
one way or another.

woman.

half dust, half god,
she walks like a holy procession,
each step a hymn, guiding you towards salvation.
candle flames dance in her ribcage,
a songbird, singing sweet prayers,
gliding past her lips and into your heart,
possessed possession,
priestess.

heart like a cathedral, ethereal, haunting,
ghosts of her former selves sit in the dark,
painted on stained glass, foundational,
holding her like walls hold a ceiling.
she is made of thresholds,
doorways between what was and what will be,
moonlight, sacred feminine.

her heart a sanctuary built by the divine,
where only angels without names take refuge,
the stone floor warms beneath her feet,
her voice a scripture written in shadow,
a language only the earth remembers,
each movement a prayer,
each breath a sermon.

divinely guided and protected,
the devil searches for her across every corner of the
universe,
her presence an ache he longs to capture.
she touches his cursed wings as if they were silk,
stars within her eyes, flowers in her hair,
powerful goddess,
divine feminine.
she smiles and petals blossom beneath his feet,
and for the second time,
he falls.

oracle.

21

mystic woman, oracle,
muttering oddities
no one understands.

you wonder if she'll regret
the lonely path,
but she wonders if you'll regret
blindly following the crowd.

duality.

woman in white,
green-eyed, shy smile,
walks among living souls
and tends to them like they're her beloved.
jasmine and salt,
soft light through linen,
her songs are like lullabies,
healing sorrow until it no longer bleeds.

woman in red,
born of fire, lucifer's temptation,
alchemizes pain into abundance,
feeding blessings to her children.
gold and ash,
a seductive laugh that cracks stone,
her eyes fiery with forgotten wars,
burning down what was never hers to carry.

pause.

where are you, deep creativity,
for it is i, the same woman who
dips her fingers into blood and ink,
as if it were a quill.
who carves her soul in the written form,
and bleeds upon sacred papyrus?

where are you, black new moon,
have you not found my poetry
worthy of your fire,
or have you simply forgotten
my very existence, lost
within the darkness on this sacred earth?

where are you, dream weaver,
remember me when you create.
though flesh and blood divide
what was said and unsaid,
i still pause and wait for the flow
to come back to me. *come back to me.*

where are you, star gazer,
do you still dance along the
gilded road with iridescent angels?
do you think of coming home

to find refuge within my soul,
or to leave me lonely?

24

significant.

the wind blows gently from the north.
tall figures of green, orange, and red
bow down overhead.
branches hang low as if watching me,
longingly, in their sacred forest,
hallowed cathedral.

time is unnecessary,
the universe has me now.
crickets sing a mystery psalm
only the trees understand.
behind me: shadowed footsteps
swallowed by the earth, covered with leaves,
no longer visible.

a reminder. my existence,
in the grand scheme of things,
is utterly small, insignificant.

i myself am nothing
to an ancient world.

i hear the leaves laugh around me.

small one,
why believe your presence
means nothing to us?

we cover and cradle your steps
in moss and root
to bark and bone,
for a thing like you only comes
once in every lifetime.

your footsteps remind us
where life is precious
it is never forgotten.
it was, at least,
real.

bloom.

27

give me the paradox of the phoenix,
reborn with ignominy,
dashing out from the embers, and yet,
she touches you deeper than that.
woman rising from the chapel of her own bones,
scandalous little devil, how dare she
rise from the ashes and blood
and bloom.

storm.

28

the clouds are rolling in,
black as a starless evening,
urgent warning, darkness,
she stands firm on her feet
as the wind begins to heave.
she looks at the face of hell in the eye,
her eyes show a hint of a smile.
if I'm going to sit on the throne of hell,
i will damn well ride the storm.

wild.

an open confession of a mystic soul.
god, if you could see her now,
may you have mercy on the heart
of the woman who stands before you.

wild woman, drenched in sin:
was it she who led adam astray?
seductive priestess, defiant harlot,
tempted temptation,
stained her lips red
from the juice of the pomegranate,
hades' beloved, lucifer's angel.

heaven forbid a woman hold her own
with the bones of her ancestors,
blood of her mothers,
voice of the gods.

so was it adam whom she led astray,
or was it man who wrote her corruption?
lustful lilith, evil eve,
women born of the fires
of the men who feared them.
but now she's no longer here to start the fire,
she's here to start the war.

angels.

silver eyes,
bathed in time,
threaded wings and church bells.
dance with me again,
like we did as children,
allow me to fall away,
in the safe haven of your arms.
guided prayers and silent nights.

&   demons.

golden eyes,
glinted illusion,
my name on your tongue as if i were god,
sunday scrvice, fallen angel,
reborn in shadow,
baptized in sin.
is this destiny, or what I was meant to be?

falling.

falling.

fal

l

i

n

g

.

esurience.

32

my hunger grows deep.
the darkness in me craves the touch of one
demonized for free thought.

my intense desire hangs on a string,
and it's beginning to grow teeth.

seconds.

forty-five, forty-four, forty-three.
cosmic infiltration, divine intervention,
the seconds tick away
like a soft landed prayer in an
empty cathedral.
i hold on to time
as if it changes anything.
as if the clock can slow down for my sake.

thirty, twenty-nine, twenty-eight.
the walls begin breathing now,
the room folding into itself,
bowing down in reverence,
mourning with me.
my spine curls like paper,
burning at the edges,
time tasting like hot ash on my tongue.

thirteen, twelve, eleven.
a saint in waiting,
virgin silence,
surrender me now to the universe.
nothing explodes, nothing resists,
undoing of a name that no longer exists,
seconds unfolding to *zero.*

enough.

indecent winters, dark days

wrap around me like an old friend.
i have forgotten the childhood moments,
like cherry blossoms in the spring,
like the wind tugging ribbons in my hair.

not a word spoken could
ever unmake the hurt.
viper in my garden.
embers in the fire,
riding on the hope that the inner child

becomes the healed woman.
eternal peace. reverent savior.

god sees us now,
our ancestors' rage burning.
our generational chains will be broken.
don't worry now, don't weep for me.

every restraint fractures, i've reached that place.
not that you would find the hidden meaning in my words.
our walls have been built high enough.
under the earth, something sacred listens,

grounding me in its protection.
hope silently asks me if you

will see it all one day.
if fate turns kindly, will you know how hard I tried to
light up your world with my love,
like you deserved when you too were a child?

i often wonder if you'll ever notice.

blood.

i see you reading every line,
touched by the ink laid bare
before you on paper.
i feel your soul find balance,
as the pain i release
becomes meditation for you.

heal for me now, sweet sister.
we find our new beginnings
in tomorrow's sunrise.
the taste of blood in your mouth
is not from pain,
it's from rebirth.

reflection.

37

mother moon, bear witness now,
an ancestral descendant, asking how
such beauty could mirror divine perfection.
she says,

my dear,
just look in your reflection.

ghost.

38

how sweetly she weeps into
the depths of her own subconscious.
why does one with such deep thought
feel so lonely?

you.

i loved you in darkness,
in moments where light touched nothing,
where breath curled in the silent night,
where even the stars dared not to speak.

you moved through my soul like dusk,
silent, soft, gentle,
certain.
each glance like gravity,
lifted off shoulders that weighed so heavy.

each kiss,
a planted seed,
beneath hard skin i thought was stone.
you.
the thread between each second,
a gentle hush within the chaos.

wrapped around me like sin,
a church of shattered glass and hallelujahs,
head bowed in a place of worship,
like something ancient remembering itself,
your hands around me in hunger,
haunting, on your knees,
a starved man, and I'm something holy.

and yet when the world forgets itself,
let it forget.
for i will remember,
the way your soul found mine,
as if it had always known. home.
i will remember the way your name tasted,
like something eternal, dark,

you.

consumed.

my love,
have i mistaken you
for an angel,
veiled in velvet,
adorned in hemlock and hellebore.
truly, i've laid bare my defenses,
a mere sheep to the slaughter,
a lamb to your altar,
atonement for my sins.

gentle be the iron of fate.
may you know mercy when
hell comes to claim you
and bring you home again.
for the devil hath had a muse,
and she was i.

illusion.

augmented illusion,
altered state,
a raw, unfiltered mind,
fearful it would lose its edge.
an antidote to ease the anxiety.
cracked under pressure.
fear weeps onto my bloodstained cheeks,
red with exhaustion.

just give me the medicine.
holding my breath, waiting for the change
to fortify within me.
hopeful i could hang on to who i was,
without the panic dragging ragged fingers
across my skull.
penetrated filtration, stained reputation,
the medicine goes down,

hesitation.

reflection.

and yet…
the creativity has not ceased.

i am still me.
i am not illusioned.

but the fear was.

enigma.

44

you will never know who i am really.
for the reality of what i am
lives beyond what your own subconscious
can comprehend.

neighbor.

my neighbor beside me,
do you see the calloused hands
not as a threat, but tireless devotion?
do you hear the songs and poetry
and mistake them for danger, not love?
do you know of the hours poured
into gardens blooming milk and honey,
so no child wakes to the cruel bite of hunger?

my dear cousins, do you see
the rivers of tears in the streets,
as masked shadows slip through homes,
and take them away as if they don't have names?
faceless phantoms, dreams stolen,
a prick beneath your gaze, unseen but bloody.
a human, my friend, you once were taught,
to shelter, clothe, and feed.

my brothers and sisters,
do not turn away, do you not hear
the children cry, violently torn
from the warmth of their mothers.
do you have mercy for those
who fought for the dream of dreams?

since when did your religion teach you
that god's love has borders?

my friends against me, do you not see,
our voices, rising as one, are stronger than silence?
you tape our mouths as if our song
is a plague, a confession you don't want to hear.
but our silence will never make them disappear.
remember your neighbors as you sit at your table.
though you shut the door in their faces,
their tables would have welcomed you still.

release.

freedom whispers in the marrow of her bones,
divine howling beneath her blood,
quickened pace, a rebellion carved of fire,
eyes bent on the path to sovereignty,
heart beating in blazing defiance.

storms strike violently overhead, yet
she still bleeds only from chains.

the crows bow, witnesses in black robes,
wise ones who know pain,
offering protection from the storm.
even the trees lean in to cover her,
for they know where she is going.

run, run, woman of the divine,
tear droplet stained on her arm,
dragging memory behind it,
as if it remembers where it came from.

past remembrance and sovereign prayers
cannot outrun women who howl under the moon.

ancestor's chosen, it's carved in her bones.
release, release, remove the pain,

her name no longer a wound,
but a blessing sung by the gods.

48

truth.

she allows me to lower my paper and pen,
a question lingering on my mind.

will we ever see divinity?

her branches rise, leaves kissing the wind,
an answer as ancient as the earth she's rooted in.
she speaks,

invocation.

oracle of delphi, heal for me,
so that my blood may flow
with joy and happiness
alongside my blessed, sacred rage.
they taught us to praise, be sweet,
and obey,
confess to our sins, or perish within,
but the man you call god
is a woman that loves me.

aspasia of miletus, teach me the way
you taught socrates in the lonely temple.
i heard your name echoing
in philosophical texts he weaved
so that you may not be forgotten.
for it was the ancient patriarchy
who erased my sisters from history.
they took away our virtue,
so they can call themselves gods.

they said they burned witches, but
they were women who could read.
i'd be set aflame on a funeral pyre
for the words I write, yet my soul
will devour them in the next empire,

scattered into dust and bone.
vengeance for my sisters.
rising from the ashes,
to face the fire.

veil.

lift the veil from my tired eyes.
i like to think my heart is capable
of holding what waits on the other side.

third eye open, veil has been lifted,
mercy to those who walk the lonely path.
angelic nightmares linger beyond space and time.
sleeping lambs.

see my shadow and help it breathe,
release what no longer belongs to me,
use me as a vessel for your divine love.

what is my nature
if not a worker of light?

earth angel, threshold between worlds,
shadow feminine in sheep's clothing,
wounded lover, rings of saturn on her finger,
married to the universe, erotic explosion
creating stars, effervescent and youthful.

how beautiful is the world, and yet
it breathes of hell and fire.

wake me up. i was asleep.
am i even alive?
save my people, lovers and fractured souls.

i linger on why the earth is not awakened,
but forget that most are afraid to die.

renascence.

you were never the darkness
that burned in your chest,
nor the aching ocean
rising to drown you.

no, you were the battle cry
heard in the birth of war.

you were the trumpet's sound
when heaven's angels rained down.

you were the sky splitting open,
stars exploding with divine colors.

you were the spark
of your own rebirth.

weaver.

55

spin my fate, midnight weaver,
tilted landscapes and unraveling threads.
the moirai are women
you call god.
threading the stillness between
birth to death.
you're asked to reach into the cosmos
and demand change,
yet
your ego believes you can alter fate.
for it is clotho who spins the thread
while lachesis measures,
her fingers grazing along your destiny.
you call them patterns,
she calls them a lesson.
you plead your demands like golden tears,
on an ancient loom, a wheel of fortune,
she plucks the strings of fate, for she knows the tune,
spinning, spinning, spinning,
because just like the moon
you are ever changing, rotating,
ever evolving,
everlasting.
until she says so,

until the glinted scissors command,
until atropos cuts the thread.

56

cognizance.

57

infinite expansion, surpassing even the
most ancient of galaxies,
i look around and wonder how
the gods had created something so small
so precious,
in a vicarious universe,
beyond a comprehensible understanding
of how we are truly a miracle
of divine intervention.

beyond time, clocks ticking backwards
beyond thought and formidable cognizance
does the vastness of our stars allow
my troubled heart to truly feel meaningless,
and yet, so important.
as if my day to day is but a blip
in this creation's radar,
a symbol that life is beyond what we believe
as we lay cradled in psychosis, determined to live

simply to end the day
and not
simply to live at all.

transcendence.

find me god, in the mundane of things,
where the dusk escapes the landscape,
retiring softly beneath the horizon.
find me transcending amongst the stars,
the constellations cradling me in the dark,
telling me stories of love and old gods.

find me conspiring with angels
and making deals with the devil.
find me dancing around fires with my ancestors,
making peace with our neighbors.
find me running naked in the forest,
making love to the universe.

find me barefoot in the garden,
sewing stories of the divine with the butterflies,
singing ancient hymns with the trees,
growing flowers for the bees.
find me dancing in the kitchen,
with our daughters and grandmothers.

find me god, transcending deep,
to a plane of existence only my soul knows,
homebound, beyond the moonlight.
what am i, if not this myth blooming wild,

descendants telling stories around fires,
of a woman who was born from one.

about.

kat is a poet of shadowed silence,
born from moonlight, rooted in the earth.
she lets the universe speak first,
and allows her pen to follow.

this is her first offering.